Membership Cube

" How to Create a Passive Income in Just a Few Simple Clicks'

I0494234

By Robert Plank
www.DoubleAgentMarketing.com

© 2016 by Robert Plank, (408) 277-0904

Section 1: Community & Overview

You're using the computer anyway. You might as well get paid for it.

I have a secret to share with you, and that's that I and thousands and thousands of other people like me are quietly but consistently making more than a full time income with this thing called Information Marketing. What we're doing is we're taking a skill, a system, a process that we know and sharing it and showing it to other people who are willing to pay money for access to that process. This can be anything from learning to play chess, losing weight, trading stocks, selling houses, learning how to play a guitar, discovering a new language, and on and on, and they are packaging their skill into a resalable offer that can sell over and over again automatically without them having to trade hours for dollars in order to get that.

I'm talking about selling digital products, but even one step beyond that, selling it inside a membership site for a bunch of different reasons. Now the first one is when you have this digital information for sale, whether that's written materials, audios or videos, you don't want to easily be compared to anyone else. Think about this question for a second - why would someone buy from you, as opposed to someone else?

Let's say for example that people want to know about excel spreadsheets, they want to know how to do their taxes and manage their personal finances. I could easily go onto sites like YouTube, sites like EzineArticles, or just search Google and other forums and collect the information together. All the information out there is basically free, now the problem with that strategy is that in my research I'll find a lot of bad or misleading information. I'll have to filter out the things that matter, things that don't matter. I'll spend tons of time trying to collect it all together, as opposed to you giving me a convenient package on how to manage my taxes and use these spread sheets, and you could even justify to me how much time and energy and money I'll save by using your process, your tools and your system.

Think about sites like Lynda.com, here is a site for one monthly fee you can gain access to a whole library of different tutorials, everything from Adobe Acrobat to Garage Bands, or to SQL Server. The reason why I would want to go to a site like that is to be able to pick through their library of the skills I need and get it all in one place in a hurry.

I run a site called Webinar Crusher, where we show people how to create content, how to present to an audience, how to build out digital classes and do it all using our special system that shortcuts the years, the trials and errors and frustration I had to go through, from how to present, how to create PowerPoint slides, how to structure things for optimal learning and performance. Think about sites like Facebook, why is it you go to sites like Facebook as opposed to someone else? Chances are because all your friends are there, there is always something interesting going on there, there's lots of traffic, and when people come to me with an idea for a crazy hare-brained site like the Membership Site, and they want to do something like become the next YouTube or become the next Yelp, or charge money to be some kind of a directory, my first question and the question you should be asking yourself is why should I buy this thing from you as opposed to someone else?

Can you basically be comparing apples to oranges to someone else's site or someone else's offer?

That all sounds well and good, so the question is what kind of stuff can you sell? What can you make a membership site about? Maybe you already have some kind of idea for some kind of information, a process or a system that you can sell or have seen other membership sites, magazines and books on different subjects like parenting, gardening, health, getting a job, investing, and so on and you thought that person teaching it is an idiot, I could completely teach a better way and I could do it a lot more effectively than this other person.

I want you to think about two things, first of all what kind of an information product, a unique solution, an easy answer that you could sell over and over again, and what kind of coaching you could give to someone if you're meeting with them once a day or once a week if not more. Now here is a unique spin on it - are you solving a desperate problem?

Here is what I mean - go to a site called ClickBank.com and click on the marketplace and scroll through the directory for the top selling information product offers out there on subjects like how to get your ex back, fat loss, dating, how to potty train your child, survival systems, how to survive at the end of the world, and online singing lessons, Paleo recipes. I'm talking about the kind of subjects where I need a quick fix now, I need to lose weight or get in shape for my high school reunion or for my wedding. I want to cure my anxiety and I want to try these hypnosis audios to do it. So this is a problem that a lot of people have, and a lot of people have tried the alternatives and they are now desperate and willing enough to try what your solution is.

Keeping in mind that this doesn't have to be some crazy thing, we have a membership site called Income Machine which shows people how to set up the different pieces they need in their online business like an opt-in page, how to choose a niche, how to have a sales letter, a download page, an auto-responder sequence, all these skills that are easy for me but hard for others, and they are in demand enough, people are willing to pay money to discover these skills and these prospects, people who are about to buy these offers have tried all the alternatives. They try the confusing plug-ins, the bloated training courses, and now they're ready to try something that's simple, easy, fast and effective.

As we're ramping up here I want you to have a few pieces of your online business in place. One is what we call a membership site which is actually very easy and very simple, and doesn't have to be some crazy piece of art that took you six months to create. We're talking about using a tool called WordPress and inside of this WordPress blog you can add in written content, videos, soft work tools, downloads, forms and communities, but this is all inside of a protected area - a membership site.

I am going to say this a few times, but get the idea out of your head that a membership site needs to be a site where someone pays month after month after month, it's simply not true, it's just a protected area where someone might be a member for free - think about sites like Facebook, someone might pay one time for these kinds of sites, or they can even pay on a recurring basis either a set number of payments or pay forever. But you want to create a membership site which is a protected area where someone can access whatever download levels they've purchased. You also want to have a sales letter in place which explains what's inside of your membership site, and you're going to want to have something called an Email Auto-Responder List, where you can email people who have not yet joined your site, email people who have quit your site, or email existing customers to get them to buy more offers.

You want to start simple and we want to avoid having a ghost-town membership and a policed membership. Here is what I mean - you don't want to have a membership site that is completely dependent on other people. You don't want to create a directory or a job site or a paid forum all on its own, because let's just say that people pay you a monthly fee to have access to a forum. What's going to happen? If anybody can post anything at anytime, you're going to have to keep checking on this site to make sure that no one takes over or spams or argues, and you're going to have to put a certain number of hours every week to keep the discussion alive, to keep things going and to keep new members coming in. It's almost a house of cards.

Now if you want to have a members area where people can post in a message board, or can leave comments under your post, that's easy and that's great because WordPress, the tool we're going to use is designed for that. What I am telling you is that can't be the center of your income. I want you to have a killer offer, to have a membership site where you solve people's problems, and this thing called community or Q&A sessions, these are bonuses. We have had a lot of fun success in creating very unique membership courses with the community's involvement.

For example, let's say you wanted to discover how to shoot different kinds of videos, product videos, sales videos, live action videos, stream-capture videos, and you had two options in front of you. One was a thick, 300 page book, and the other option was a very thin, 30 page manual, but both of these things had the exact same information inside of them. 300 page book, 30 page thin manual, exact same information - of course you'd choose the easier option. Now what if you had that 30 page book but you also had the choice to either read the book, the thin book or watch videos on how to actually do these things? Instead of just having to read some text you could see these things in action, you could see how to set up the lights around you, how to choose the perfect video camera, how to use the software to edit a video - it was actually shown to you instead of having to read it. Of course, if I told you that both things contained similar information, you'd choose the video because it would be easier to take in that information.

Keep this in mind, when we are all starting out we just want money and we get crazy with the pencil and paper and the calculator and we tell ourselves, if only I got 1000 members at $10 a month that would equal this level of income, and you can't guarantee that, but what you can do is stack that in your favor by creating something that's appealing to people who are already looking for the answer that you provide. If we can choose a desperate problem, if we can model our offer after what other people are doing but make ours better, and better might mean faster, slimmer or with extra tools or resources like this community, we could put it inside a membership site and we've already made huge strides and huge progress towards this passive online recurring income by trading our knowledge for dollars instead of our time for dollars.

You don't want to have a ghost-town where no one posts or a policed state where everyone posts, instead you want to solve people's problems and add on extra goodies and gimmicks. Goodies and gimmicks are things like drip content. It is possible for you to create a members area, a download area where someone joins and they might pay onetime or it might be on a monthly basis and they get videos and content and different things dripped out to them over time.

You could use a membership site to sell more than one item, for example, if you have three different courses on how to play the drums. You could sell all three from the same site and if someone wanted to buy all three at once, the access they see is all that content. If they only want to buy one of the courses then they login and they only see those specific videos and reports, and if they want to buy the other level, they can do that within the same member's area. This makes it very easy for you, because you don't have to maintain multiple sites and you can quickly and easily have a bird's eye view of who has access to which of your sites and which of your products.

Another great thing about creating a membership site is that it stays evergreen. I could create a course on how to record different kinds of video, put it in a membership site and sell that for years and years until I decide to update the training. The next thing I want you to consider is what would be the dream all in one dashboard for you to use if you were first starting out? If you were first getting into weight loss, what would be the ideal scenario where you went to a web page and you looked at a grid of three boxes across and three boxes down, so nine squares total, and you could just click on whichever box was important for you on that day. Maybe we're talking about a meal plan where on different days of the week or different days of the month there were certain foods to be eaten, or on different weeks or different types of days you could do a diet one day or an exercise a different day, or different kinds of exercises or different kinds of diets, but it was just a one-stop all in one shop, a dashboard for someone to use on a daily basis, have a daily resource where even if someone only paid one time or someone has only paid a few payments, or they bought years ago, they could still login now today, years later, and still use this daily resource.

I want you to get a membership site up and running and online right now today so that you don't have to be compared with other competitors in your niche, so that you can easily place and upload and update information products and tell your buyers about new offers or about updates, and give them a convenient place to log back in and consume your products. I want you to use a membership area as a protected download area for you to share your process and your system, whether that is presented in videos or written materials, where you want something that solves people's problems and isn't necessarily a knock-off of sites like YouTube and Twitter.

I want you to have the bare basics of a membership site set up so that you can add on extras such as drip or extra products, or to create a whole entire dashboard.

Section 2: Single Payment Sites

One problem, one solution. That's the attitude I want you to have, going forward, as you create your basic, most simple form of your membership site. I can't tell you how many conversations I've had with someone about their upcoming membership site.

For example, how to lose weight, and I asked, "What kind of weight loss membership site are you about to put out?" They tell me they've got different kinds of software programs ready to go, accountability systems, charts and graphs, different videos and reports, and it turns out that they've spent six months, a year, two years, or even longer making this product just right, creating all kinds of content, tons of research, outsourcers, proofreaders, editors, and they spent two years with no idea whether the marketplace even wants this product or maybe the marketplace wanted it when they first started on it, but things have changed in two years.

When someone tells me about, for example, their weight loss site, my immediate question is, "When I join your site, what do I get immediately, what do I get in the first seven days, and what do I get in the first 21 days?"

More often than not, they don't have an answer for me, but if you do have an answer, then you'll be on track to create and finish and have a membership site up and running, way faster than your competitors.

Let's be honest, everyone has an idea. Most people can't see it through to completion. We're going to dial up your web browser to a site like Amazon.com and check out the bestseller lists and scroll through and maybe look into some of the different categories to filter out the fiction titles, and I'm seeing things like "The Super Shred Diet," "Jim Kramer's Get Rich Quickly," "The Daniel Plan," - that's more weight loss.

Let me check a couple of categories, like Business and Investing, Computers and Technology, Health, Fitness, and Dieting, and Self Help to see what bestsellers come up. I'm seeing "Thinking Fast and Slow," "Get Big Fast and Do More Good," lots of books about the Kindle Fire, about the iPhone, Windows 8.

We might scroll through and get a few ideas – for example, "The Happiest Baby on the Block," "What to Expect When You're Expecting," ideas for books. But let me really quick touch about a handful of types of books that won't work very well as products, and ones that will actually work very well.

You might see that some company online sells t-shirts, and you'll say, "Great, I want to make a t-shirt company." The problem with that is there's a lot of upfront costs for you, it's really tough to differentiate yourself, compared to running an information business.

Now, let's talk about a couple of information businesses that aren't sexy, that you wouldn't realize at first. For example, you might find that there are books out there on how to get a high score on the SAT, or how to study well, or get good grades, or do well in college.

The problem, though, is that this isn't an exciting or desperate need. Even though these kinds of books might sell well, think about who's buying them: mostly parents of students, and they're not spending hundreds of dollars, or hundreds of dollars per month, to get access to this information.

Now, what about different hobby types of niches? Well, these are really hit or miss. For example, there's a membership site called Dollar Shave Club, and basically they send a razor in the mail every month to you, and they just barely make a profit, or even lose money, until they have a certain amount of customers every single month.

You might hear about this membership site in the news, and the site you're going to also mail shaving kids to people every single month, or create lots of videos and tips about how to shave better, but it just doesn't seem that exciting and it's not like I'm losing sleep on how well or how poorly I'm shaving this particular week.

Now, on the other hand, if we're talking about things like pregnancy, parenting, relationships, there's definitely something there if you can find your own angle, because people are willing to spend a lot of money, especially when you're going the selling angle of comparing your solution to the cost of divorce, the cost of a therapist, the cost of all the self help books you've tried already.

When we're talking about a lot of these areas, and I'm thinking even about back to the weight loss niche, how we can cut through all the crap and position ourselves as the breath of fresh air, as the very simple, the easy fix, one problem, one solution kind of membership site.

Think about the infomercials you see on TV or the books you hear about over and over on Amazon, but be sure to filter out the topics that aren't sexy. That's why I say in the ClickBank earlier, to find those really hot button topics that are really sexy.

Now, let me throw a couple other ideas at you. What if you were some kind of an expert on, for example, back pain, and you said, "Here's my membership site on how to fix your back pain. It requires this kind of yoga, exercise, acupuncture, diets, who knows what," but you have some kind of system to solving someone's back pain.

Well, what's the problem here? The problem is that there's probably only one ebook that you can sell somebody, on how to fix their back pain. You say, "Here's my process for fixing your back pain, a ten dollar ebook and that's it." Now, once their back pain is fixed, there's really nothing else you can sell to them from that point forward.

Even though we have different levels here, there are things that people sell left and right, but aren't a good idea for you to get into. Then there's some niches we can filter out that aren't sexy or aren't desperate needs, and then we can take this one step further and remove niches where there's no future.

Now, if you think about things, like guitar and golf, there's a future in those niches, because if you can teach someone how to become good at the guitar very quickly, then you can teach new techniques on chords or how to compose your guitar songs, or you can sell them on the back end of different kinds of picks and guitars, guitar strings, tuning devices.

There's definitely a future and there's definitely multiple courses that you can create in the guitar niche. Now, let's say we're thinking about it this way. In whatever niche you're thinking of, is it possible – and I don't want you to list them, but is it possible that there are ten different courses that you could possibly create that are priced at $100 or at $1000?

If the answer is yes, then there's tons of room for you to grow, especially if you find that you can branch out into other products in the same niche. For example, in the golf niche, you could make a product on how to improve your golf game, even if you're a pro, a golf product on how to improve your distance or how to improve your accuracy, or a certain kind of golfing, or how to win some kind of golf tournament.

Well, this whole time, we're thinking about the solution to a desperate problem, and this will help you avoid another trap that so many membership site creators fall into, and it's this idea of tip overload.

They think that you can make a site about any niche, whether it's boring, whether there are no buyers in it, and just overload people with tips and charge ten bucks a month for one tip a day or one article a week or one interview a month, and I'm here to tell you that there's no future for you in that.

But there is a future in having this idea of a 30-day, 20-day, 10-day boot camp, and posing the question to yourself, If someone was going to pay me $1000, if someone was in a really desperate position in guitar playing, in golf playing, in learning the piano, in weight loss and stock trading, and they were paying me $1000 one time to fix all their problems in twenty days, what would I fix for them right now? What would I fix for them in the first week, in the second week, in the third week?

Then, don't think about things past that twenty day period, because it's up to you to create a one problem, one solution, self-contained, single payment site, put it out there, test the marketplace, and your community and your buyers and your prospects and your list will tell you what to create next.

But we don't want to plan out our entire future, we don't want to map out the next ten products or the next ten membership sites, or the next ten months of membership content.

Let's just create twenty days, or even just one day of a problem solving system to help people out. What we're going to do is create a series of, let's just say, four videos, and place them inside of our membership site.

Now, we're going to set up WordPress and Wishlist Member, and then place a sales letter online. For this, we can use a plugin called Paper Template, and then a payment processing service, called PayPal, and create a button that people can click on to then pay us money.

They go through the checkout the process and enter in their credit card details for, say, $100, so they go to our sales letter, they see the payment button, they click on that button, they check out, and fill in their credit card details for $100, then check out and then create an account in our membership site that they can use to log in again and again, if they ever want to go back and watch the videos or see them again or re-update the videos with something new, or they come back years later and want to check in on the purchase. That is always online.

The great thing about using an autopilot membership site is that if someone refunds the money and when someone makes a digital purchase from you online, it's very easy for them to do that, but luckily this percentage is very, very low.

But on the off chance they do refund, it cuts off their access and they can no longer log in to your membership site on that particular level they paid for, which means that they will not be able to access the purchase they refunded.

That means that if they paid and you kept the money, they have access to what they paid for. If they paid and they take the money back, they no longer have access. This makes a membership site – remember, a membership site is not necessarily a site where someone pays month after month, but it can be.

But if we have this membership site that's a protected area, even if it's as simple as someone paying us $100 one single time, it becomes very easy to mange ten, twenty, 100, 1,000, 10,000 members in one single place.

Now, our goal for this short term is to build a list of buyers. Maybe you've heard the saying, "The money is in the list," or you've heard about companies and startups, like Squidoo or Twitter, that pile up hundreds of thousands of users, of free users, but still, they're people who have registered for this kind of site.

I'm here to tell you that the best kind of members you can have registered in your site are the ones that have paid you money. Even if they've only paid you one time, or they've only paid you ten dollars or a hundred dollars, that's far, far more valuable than someone who hasn't paid you any money, for a lot of reasons.

If someone's paid you even ten dollars, you now know a ton of things about them. First of all, they own a credit card and know how to use it and are comfortable using it online, and are comfortable using it online with you, and that they're passionate enough about this niche to spend money.

Once they've made that first initial purchase, they're way more likely to make purchases again and again and again. Now, why am I putting everything in such simple terms, $100 one time, twenty days or less, four videos? Because I don't want you to get burned out.

I fell into this trap early on, and everyone I know who's gone down the membership site route made this mistake, of thinking too big, wanting to take over the world, and they plan and pile up and they create hundreds of pages of content, or dozens of videos, and even worse, they might set up some kind of monthly site where now they've promised to deliver new tips, new content, new videos month after month after month, and six months later, they're now burned out.

Now, I have this revelation when I first saw a membership site, about this thing called copy-writing, which is writing persuasive language to place on print ads and on web pages, to get people to buy.

Now, it sounds great, right? You pay $100, or you pay $200 a month, to get access to all these interviews from the world's greatest living – and some dead – legends of copywriters.

The problem, though, is that the sales letter advertising the membership site had a phrase in there that said something like, "By the end of the second month, you'll be able to create your own sales letter," and I was thinking that the end of the second month – basically I have to buy now, and then wait over two months just to have this thing that I wanted to have yesterday, that I want to have today, or this week, if possible.

Now, here's another problem, is let's say that you've created six months of content, and you say, "Well, here's all this stuff." First of all, you have to list all these different things that I'm paying for. Now, what if what's coming up in six months is fantastic and it's the whole reason for joining this monthly membership site?

The problem is, I have to wait six months to get access to it. Then you might say to me, "Well, you know what? What's coming in six months isn't that important. It just builds on what was there before," and I'm thinking, "Well, now I shouldn't even stay in for six months."

Instead of trying to nickel and dime yourself, or instead of trying to race to this free level, instead of trying to work so hard for this ten dollar a month site, just send someone something for $100 one time, and sell something to them once per year.

This might be a different product or an upsell or an updated version of the product you have, but instead of thinking in terms of five dollars a month or ten dollars a month, or something has to be monthly, let's make it simple for now, and decide what can we charge a single payment for, keeping in mind that we can always create new stuff, we can always create bundle offers, or even split up the payments and the payment plans and stretch this thing out for three months, five months, ten months later on, if this solution we put out is a hit with our marketplace.

You might be noticing that I use these terms like "membership site," "product," "solution," all interchangeably, and you should, too. Don't think of a membership site as this huge, giant project. Think of it as a solution to people's problems.

This is great because now you don't have to cut out ten hours a week, or ten hours a month of your schedule to generate all this new content. You don't have to find yourself scraping the bottom of the barrel to think of new tips and ideas, or pilot new interviews, so now you can't even describe what's inside your membership site because it has so many things.

You can instead focus on the base hits. Create this solution, figure out the best way to present it, and then tweak and test and just focus on getting ten people, 100 people, and filling this membership site up with single payment buyers.

You want to keep things simple, and here's another thought to put in your head. Remember how before we said that any information on the internet is freely available? If you have a membership site all about how to play a guitar, sure, I can go out and I can go to a bookstore and I can buy all kinds of guitar books.

I can nickel and dime myself and buy all kinds of five dollar PDF books about guitar. I can watch YouTube videos, I can read articles, I can browse forums, but what does that get me? A giant mess.

Your membership site is the simplicity everyone's been looking for. All of the information that people want is consolidated, it's compressed into one single package, where now they can, instead of spending a year on research, six months on trial and error, six months on practice, now they can master the guitar in seven days or less, just by going through some simple milestones.

Let's focus on how you can consolidate all the noise into one place and leave out the things that don't matter, emphasize the speed. Someone shouldn't have to pay you month after month after month to get the latest guitar tip. They shouldn't have to keep paying you so that they can finally play their first song at the end of three months.

Is it possible to show someone, to teach someone, even across the internet, how to play the guitar by this time tomorrow night, or in twenty minutes, can they at least play some kind of guitar? Use your imagination on this.

For example, I've seen some kind of a device that fits over a guitar, where it changes the finger position someone has to use to create chords, and it's just pushing one of four colored buttons.

Now, you don't even have to create this device. Just send someone a copy of this, by buying it for them on Amazon, or give them a link on Amazon to buy it for themselves, but base your training around this device, so that now, if someone is looking for a shortcut, you've given it to them, and it's much more valuable than them just buying the device on its own.

You can show them what guitar to get, what kind of pick to get, this device to get them started, which songs to focus on, which chords to focus on, and just the bare essentials, the bare minimum to get them to this goal as fast as possible.

Lance Tomashiro and I like to call this goal-based training, where if you have your 20 or 21 day course, and you have a milestone, and you have four different modules, then we're trying to figure out, in this first module, when someone is first getting started, we want them to reach a certain goal in sixty to ninety minutes.

We want to show them how to get started quickly, how to get some easy results, and then give them an assignment or a challenge, at the end of this training course, at the end of this module, so that they can watch the sixty or ninety-minute presentation, figure out what needs to be done, and actually do it themselves.

That way, they get results. That way, you are now differentiated from all the other videos, books, and courses out there. Now you're the one that finally gets them the results. They buy right now, they watch that first module, they see that tonight, and then they get that first result.

Now, here's what I really like to do with single payment sites, is to completely ignore any idea about drip content just yet. They pay me one time, they get four modules, and they get them all at once, and then they can go through them as fast or as slow as they want, but they get everything at once.

They buy this four module guitar course for $100, and tonight they go through module one, and have their assignment or, for example, they might learn four chords or they might learn one particular song that they can now play with these guitar techniques that they've discovered from you. That's module one. That's tonight.

Then, in seven days, they get to that next milestone, that next logical step. Maybe they figure out a couple of extra songs to play. Maybe on module three, which is now on day fourteen, they discover how to read music or how to do rhythm or some other advanced topic.

Then in module four, which is now on day 21, they now know how to play some more advanced songs and know certain ways to play with other players, or things about how to perform as a guitarist, but something that now wraps it all together.

By adding these rules, these constraints, we've now eliminated many of our choices and we just figure out how to make our unique, exciting solution fit into this structure we've created.

It's four modules, $100, they get everything at once, but your training is designed to give them module one up front, when they first join, with an assignment. Module two should logically be completed after seven days with an assignment, although they can skip ahead or take longer if they want.

Module three, on day fourteen, again with an assignment, and then module four on day 21. What you have are four logical modules – now, four is a great number because it's not too many.

It's not like they're getting 50 videos of two minutes each, they're not getting ten modules where they have to basically put everything aside all month and only focus on your course. They get four easy modules.

That means that if they only have one or two hours per week to devote to your course, then great. They can still make use of it. It's easy, it's powerful, but it's not an overload. We consolidated it all at once, and besides the speed, and this is goal-based training.

The structure I like to use, if I'm still stuck about whatever topics I'm talking about, is this: the first module, what they should be going through the night they join is the quick start.

We don't want to have an intro or an overview video, we want to give them results fast. We want to show them how to run that first webinar, create that first membership site, upload and post that first video, have that membership site online, or in your case, play the guitar quickly and play their first song, go to the driving range and get their first hole in one or hole in less than four hits.

If you're teaching real estate, how to choose which house they are going to use to do a quick flip. Whatever it is, that first module is the quick and easy result. Now, the second module is going to be the bigger result, but it's going to be the main hook for your course, the huge thing that just really draws people in.

It might be that, at first, they figured out how to play the guitar, but now module two will be, out of all the guitar songs, here are the top five songs that are ever played or ever requested, and you're going to show them how to play all five of them in this module.

They don't have to learn everything and everything there is about guitar, but because you've taught a couple of pieces to it, here's where this simple piece now fits into this bigger result.

Module two is the bigger, but fun result, and this is the main reason they bought the course. Having that quick start, that simple jump start is fine, but now they have this big result.

I'm thinking back to a course on WordPress we sold years ago, where the first module was just how to get WordPress set up. The second one was this huge WordPress sales letter plugin.

We have a four module podcasting course, and the first module is just how to record a quick five minute audio program for an internet radio show and get the program submitted, and then the second module is how to record a full, twenty minute program, with all the best bells and whistles and music and formatting, and that is the main reason people buy.

Module one is the quick result, module two is what they want, and then module three is what they really need, and the things that, when you get to this level, you can't really ignore that.

Now you have to discover and use things like rhythm and reading music, keeping in mind that we're still making it fun and still not trying to create a list of tips, we're not trying to create an exhaustive encyclopedia.

We're taking people from one fun adventure to the next, and that might mean, in most cases, that we present things almost a little bit out of order. We gave them this quick jump start, we snuck in a couple things that they really want, and then now we can back up and backtrack and do these things we really need.

For example, in our podcasting course, you might talk about traffic. In our membership course, we might back up a little bit and talk about how to market to your membership site. In our webinar course, the first call and modules might be about how to sell a bunch of people into a class, and now it's time to actually fulfill that class.

This third module, as you're almost winding the four modules down, we're talking about the thing that they really need, but we still need to find a way to make it fun and sexy and have an interesting hook.

Finally, the fourth module is some blend of wrapping things up, tying up loose ends, things that didn't really fit anywhere else, and then some kind of behind the scenes or case study or critique.

Once again, we want to avoid the high school essay mentality. We don't want to have that intro, overview module with the history of the guitar, and we also want to avoid, at the end, we don't want to have the conclusion. We don't want to recap or retread the old things.

We want to just wrap up those loose ends and fit in whatever slightly more advanced topics that didn't work anywhere else. There's four modules. The first one is the quick start, the second one is what they want, the third one is what they need, and the fourth one is loose ends, critiques, behind the scenes, case studies.

Now, as you're moving forward, something I want to put in your head is that the membership site needs to be up and running and online as quickly as possible. That way, we can begin selling it, we can begin marketing it, we can send traffic to it, and we can figure out if people are buying, why they're buying – and it's usually not the reason you think.

Then we can emphasize that more, we can do more of that, and if they're not buying, then we can readjust. So many times I see people spend years and years getting the content just right, and then when the site doesn't start selling right out of the gate, they give up and now those two years have been wasted.

Instead of wasting two years, spend a few hours or a couple of days on these videos, on this content, on the setup, and then we can get to these things like setting up a sales letter and marketing.

Now, a few things about that. First of all, people missed the point about their public-facing web pages. What you should do – and we're going to be getting to this in a little while – is set up your membership site, whatever your domain is, .com/members. You can always register a .com domain name at a site called NameCheap.com.

Then get your website hosted at a webhost called HostGator.com. Now, when someone types in the name of your website, like backpaincrusher.com or superduperguitarcourse.com, they end up on a website that you pay a monthly fee for, and that you host and that you have total control over.

This should be your sales letter. When someone goes to superduperguitarcourse.com, they end up on a web page where you explain a few things. You explain what brought them to this web page, and usually out of frustration, usually got other alternatives, things that didn't work.

You explain to them what your course is and why it's in their best interests to buy right now, keeping in mind what's in it for them. No one cares about you. No one cares about how much you've struggled or how long you've spent creating this course, or how much it cost you.

I care about the problems that you can solve for me. We want to be careful in the words we use, especially, so that we explain things in a really fun and exciting way, even if we're not talking about the most fun topic ever.

For example, with real estate, what kind of scenarios or stories or things that maybe you have done in the past can we emphasize?

Maybe if, in the past, you saw that beat up old house down the block that was just sitting there and sitting there and sitting there, and one day you decide to do something about it.

Because of your real estate skill, you went in and got some kind of loan, got the house, fixed it up in a week, and you'd made $20,000 and sold the house to a brand new family of four, and now it's the coolest, cleanest looking house on the block.

If you're talking about guitar, maybe you could tell a story about how you were at a party or you were at a club one night, and people were playing guitar, it was open mic night, and you said, "You know, I'll play a little bit," and everyone laughed at you, but then you just rocked the house.

We can do all these sales triggers and do things that basically get people excited to have your product in their hands, so to speak, even though it's 100 percent digital, we're not even getting to mailing a physical item in the mail just yet. They're just buying the information.

They're buying the videos, the reports, the things that they can read on the computer or print out or watch on their tablet or any kind of device, but we're focusing not so much on the mechanics or the metrics or it's got fifty hours of video, or this is an 180-page report.

We want to compare apples to oranges. You want to be in your own category, separate from everyone else. We want people to get excited about getting access to your course. What results will they have?

What will they be able to do in just a few minutes or a few hours of having access to your system and your training, that they've been frustrated with maybe even their entire lives, leading up to this point?

You want to be careful about the things that we say, and even if you're stuck and even if you don't have a lot to say about selling to people in your course, just think for now about ten good reasons why people would want access to your course, ten things that they can get, and things that they get aren't things that they learned.

By the way, I don't even like to use the word learned. I like to use the word like discover, or breakthrough, or uncover. What kind of things will they do after they've discovered how to play the guitar?

Not necessarily you'll learn different chords, you'll learn these things, but we can say, "After you've discovered how to play such and such chord, you'll play any song by ear in five minutes," if that's something that could happen, or, "You could instantly shortcut the next five years of guitar instruction," or, "You can skip fifty lessons that you'd have to go through in-person guitar instruction."

You know what's also helpful here? When you're thinking about the sales letter and the marketing and things like that, is look at your competitors. I know that early on, I winced every time I thought about someone else that might be in my space, but you know what?

Those are where you're going to get your best ideas from, not copying, not imitating, but just ideas here and there. If you notice that every single guitar sales letter on ClickBank plays an audio clip of their guitar training, or if they all use certain words or certain phrases, or if they all cover certain areas of playing the guitar, you can just build a better mousetrap, so to speak.

Create this thing called a sales letter, think about what's in it for them, ten good reasons why they'd want to buy, be sexy and careful with the words. The next thing is that order really matters when it comes to these things like sales letters.

We're basically making an argument where you want people to come to your sales letter and their first reaction is, "Finally I'm in the right place," and their last reaction is, "I should have bought this a year ago. I can't buy this fast enough."

We want to get them from Point A to Point B, and order really matters here. We want to start off with the problem, what brought them there, so they know they're in the right place, that this is the perfect solution for them, introduce that solution, which is your membership site.

Then go into detail about the different modules and what they'll discover, once they are a member, and then what to do right now, here's what you get. I really recommend that you explain these four modules in sexy terms, and in the future, if you can think of three easy bonuses that you can add in – we'll get to that in a little while, but bonuses such as if there's a piece of software that you can buy the rights to or include, that'll help them, or a checklist, or a quick start guide, or even a one on one coaching that will help just accelerate what they have, and it'll be light years ahead of any book or dvd that you might buy for ten bucks.

This is just incomparable to what they'd get anywhere else. Something to think about here is that if you eliminate all of the other possibilities of what to next to solve their current problem, and the only remaining option is to use you, that's a pretty dang compelling sales argument.

Their options, if they're thinking about playing guitar, is to not learn it at all, and they'll always wish they learned, is to keep trying what they've been doing now, which might be learning on their own, which is very frustrating, or going and meeting a guitar instructor in person, which means that it's very expensive every single time, and it's very time consuming and it's frustrating in its own way.

Another option would be to maybe buy some other course, buy some five dollar ebook, but that will just leave them more confused than they are right now. Finally, what they really should do is just join your course because it's all in one place, it all has video, it has your system, you've taught X number of students and guess what?

If you're just buying this course right now, it's cheaper than one single guitar lesson, but even taking into account gas and travel and waiting, just get this once and now your problem is solved forever.

The secret for you is that even though you've solved this initial problem, later on in the future, you'll be able to solve other problems for them, but a huge breakthrough I had – and this is important – is that the majority of the buyers you're going to have are newbies.

I know we don't like to think that we teach these crazy advanced concepts, but in reality, most people just want the simple things figured out. They just want to lose ten pound. They just want to live ten years longer.

They just want to go from a newbie at golf to being an average golf player, and that's not to say we can't make more products in the future, but just think about the majority of your prospects and your buyers are going to be newbies.

Let's start off and keep things simple and rush our membership site to the market, just because you don't know what's going to be a big hit and what's going to be a flop, so you need to get that membership site out there quickly, so that you can readjust, make a single payment site, price it at $100, model it after the best selling books, ClickBank products, and other membership sites you see when you're doing your searches, keeping in mind that a membership site does not have to be reoccurring, and for the purposes of us getting something set up and up and running quickly, it should just be a single payment site where they just pay you $100, where they get all four modules at once, but you've given them a structure for them to follow, of them going to the first module, seeing what there is to uncover.

They complete the assignment or the challenge, and then go on to the next and the next and the next. Now they have crossed these four milestones to get to this huge goal in just 21 days or less.

Section 3: Management & Setup

Forget right now about starting a site from scratch. I do not want you to do it. Instead, I want to share with you the exact tools that I used and that you will use to create your very own moneymaking autopilot membership site.

The next thing is stop being overwhelmed with all of the possibilities. I am not here to give you 10 different possible webhosts, 20 different possible membership site platforms. I am here to give you a plan that is proven, that works, that you can use on plugin and make your own.

Do you want to know where to get your dotcom domain hosted? Namecheap. Web host? HostGator. What to use to hold the content in your site? WordPress. How to process payments? PayPal. How to protect the contents so that only paying members get access? WishList Member.

I want you to use those tools, and the great thing about tools such as WordPress and WishList Member, is they both have add-ons. If you want to change the design of your membership site, you just install a different WordPress theme and everything will be completely different. If you want to add a forum or a popup to your membership site, you just install a plugin and you can add on to it.

I want you to think for one second about something called the "iceberg" principle. If you are out there on the ocean and you see an iceberg, a big chunk of ice out there in the water, it looks really tiny. The reason for this is because 90% of the iceberg is actually under water. This is why ships crash into them because they only see the tiniest topmost peak of it.

This is also true when you look at a website. When you are looking at a website, looking at any kind of product that is out there for sale, you see that 10%, but the 90%, the positioning, testing, tweaking, trying to figure out what to name things, adding graphics, creating content, getting traffic, filing it up with members, getting it selling over and over again, that is the part you do not see.

That is why it is nearly impossible for anyone on the internet to exactly copy anyone. That is why if you have a functioning and working internet business, you are almost copy-proof because people will copy the wrong things from you.

The iceberg principle, as it relates to you and your membership site is this, 10% is your membership site and your sales letter, the other 90% are all the long-term activities that you do once that site is established, mostly list building, traffic building, testing, and tweaking. Once again, the average person never gets passed that initial 10%.

They spend their entire internet career plotting, scheming, brainstorming, creating content, making everything perfect, and it never gets to the part where they actually have to market and promote the website. That is why I want you to get that side of up and running an online as fast as possible. That way we can get to the 90% of actually growing and building an online business.

Let me walk you through what we are going to do in order to get your membership site up and running an online. We are going to use your web host control panel. Most of them have an area called cPanel. In that, there is an area called Fantastico.

You will use that to install a piece of software called WordPress. Here is what I like to do. I would like to register a brand new domain name using Namecheap, park it on a web host using HostGator. Then, install WordPress and the top level root of the site.

Then, I use a plugin of ours called PaperTemplate to add a piece of paper look and feel where I can quickly add some headlines and bullet points explaining this thing that they will be buying membership access to. Then I create the membership site. I create a second WordPress blog in the members' folder of the site. If your site is example.com, we are going to create a sales letter at the root, so when someone types example.com they see that sales letter.

Then, we are going to create a second separate WordPress installation in the members' folder at example.com/members. Once again, using this tool called cPanel and Fantastico, we can then install a second blog entirely at example.com/members, and in this members WordPress site, we install a plugin called WishList Member.

A WishList Member is cool because it allows you to create accounts for 10, 100, 10,000 or 100,000 of your paying members. They can log in and view whatever content you have available to them. But, in order to log in, they have to already have an account or pay you using your sales letter to get access to this. I am going to talk about that in a few minutes.

The next thing I want to share with you is the idea of levels. The thing that makes WishList Member unique from every other membership plugin out there is the ability to have a lot of add-ons, and is this idea of levels. What I like to do is I created new membership site, create a level called "Full" and protect every single page and post inside of that WordPress site.

What does this mean? It means when someone buys from me, they buy access to this thing called the Full level. This Full level has access to every piece of content in the site. They logged out, they see nothing, they pay or they log in, they see everything.

Then we can get to the advanced stuff after this, like adding in a payment button, using drip content. That is the idea of getting your WordPress membership site online. Get your domain web host. Install a sales letter at the root of your domain.

Install a second WordPress installation in the members' folder of your domain. Install a WishList Member on top of WordPress. Add in levels. Create a payment button to connect your sales letter to your membership site, and then get to the more advanced stuff like drip.

By the way, we have a training course at membershipcube.com, where we will walk you through all these steps and buy WishList Member for you, and include lots of other plugins, themes, tools, and resources that we use on a daily basis for our membership site.

The first thing you want to do is go into your cPanel area. Whatever your domain name is, like example.com. Go to example.com/cpanel. This will give you a screen with lots of icons to do anything and everything from setup email folders to add patch domains or sub-domains, but the important part is to find an area that is as fantastically, click on the icon to go to the WordPress section and is a new WordPress installation.

Now, you are going to see a form that you could fill out and enter things such as the exact place you want this WordPress site setup, and what username and password you are going to use for you personally to log in to this site as the administrator. Be sure to write this one down for safe keeping.

After that is all done, you can always go back and log in to the site like going to whatever the WordPress site is /wp-admin. When you set up the WordPress site at the root of your domain, you go to Fantastico, choose the domain name you want to install it on. Usually, you just have the one, choose to not install at any folder because you want it at the root.

For the username, I usually put my first and last name like Robert Plank. For the password, I choose a hard to guess password with both letters and numbers that I also would not forget. Once that site is setup, you can go to example.com/wp-admin and then log in and once you are there, you will see bare boned WordPress site, where you can add in pages or post, but what we are going to do is install our plugin called PaperTemplate, which you can pick up if you want at PaperTemplate.com.

Go to plugins, add new upload in WordPress, and upload the zip file we give to you as part of PaperTemplate, and this new plugin will then allow you to go to the PaperTemplate menu on the side bar and is a new landing page, and then type in the headline you want, the bullet points you want, and save it and set is as the front most page of your site.

Now, when someone goes to example.com, they have nothing else to do other than see the place where you have advertised, jazzed up, hyped up, and explained your membership site. That is the frontend, that is your sales letter. Then, you can go to cPanel once again, example.com/cpanel. Go to Fantastico once again, WordPress new installation, but this time you want to install your second WordPress site in the members folder.

Once again, fill in the username and password you want. I recommend you keeping the same one so that way you do not have to remember multiple usernames and passwords. This will be your membership site. This will be where you will have all your backend contents.

Once again, your sales letter, your public webpage is at example.com. But all your private membership content is at example.com/members. Once you have this /members blog setup, it is a very similar process to log in. Go to example.com/members/wp-admin and you will see your screen where you can once again enter your username and password and get access once again to your WordPress dashboard.

You install the WishList Member plugin which we give to you as part of Membershipcube. Go to wishlistmember.com to grab your copy and you go to plugins, add new upload and upload the zip file containing the WishList Member plugin, and they will have you log in to their customer area to grab what is called your license key. Once that is set up, you will be ready to use install WishList Member.

At this point, I really would not recommend messing with any other plugins. By the way, you can add by going to plugins, add new. You do not need to figure out your design or your theme just yet. You choose by going to the appearance tab. For now, just add your initial posts and pages.

I will only explain this part really quick. WordPress originally was meant as a journaling or blogging software which means you will go to the site, click on, add new post, and type in a new diary entry. For example, a post on January 1, February 1, March 1 and so on.

Those are posts. Those are journal entries that go from top to bottom on your WordPress blog and with usually the most recent one at the top. Technically, you could create a site in a WordPress, add just one post to it, sell access to that, and as you added new posts, you would just add them by going to post, add new and the people would log in and they would see the most recent post at the very top.

Now, you might also want to add these things called pages for extra reference and bonus materials. Let us think about this for a second. You know how some sites have an "About Us" page or some sites have a "Contact Us" page. Those do not really fit as diary journal type entries. Those are things that go from left to right in the top side bar.

So, the difference between posts and pages is that posts are more like diary entries where they usually have a date attached to them and they go from bottom to top. Pages are more like the navigation of your site or the content of the site where they do not have any kind of date attached to them and they are more of standalone areas of your site.

To start off and to keep things simple, I would highly recommend you to limit yourself to just post for now. Go to post, add new, and type in whatever content you want from module one or record a video and upload it to YouTube, and copy and paste the YouTube link to your members area. That is good enough for now until you decide later to reorganize.

Just a recap, we have used your cPanel Fantastico area of your webhost backend to install WordPress at the root of your domain with PaperTemplate, then we install WordPress in the members' folder, with WishList Member, and then we have created one or two post of content to protect.

Now, we want to move on to WishList Member and a couple of quick things you want to do. You want to add at least one level, you want to protect the content and assign it to that level. We want to add the ability for our members to log in and log out. And then we want to add the ability to take payments and set up a button on our frontend sales letter, that way people can join our site.

There might be some new unfamiliar screens or terminology if you have not done this before but it is all very simple. The first thing I would like to do as I said is after installing WishList Member and entering in my license key, I add in a membership level called Full. I just go to the levels tab in WishList, add in a level called Full and give it access to everything, all posts, all categories, all pages, all content. This one level has access to the entire site.

The next thing I want to do with WishList Member is go to the settings tab, and check the box to only show content for each membership level. This ensures that when we protect our content in a minute, that it is going to be shielded from the outside world.

Be sure to save your changes then go to content and go to the dropdown that says content protection, and you will see some check boxes next to your module one post or next to any other content on the site.

You want to make sure that these are all checked. This was to make sure that if someone has logged out of your site, that they would not see this content, but if someone has logged in if they are member, they do see this content. Make sure those are checked and click on set protection. Now, your posts are sheltered from the outside world.

You can test this for yourself like going to the site, like going to example.com/members. Because you are still logged in, you should still be able to see all the posts that are in front of you. But as soon as you click on the log out link, now the entire site is gone.

You might notice something. When you view the frontpage of your site, once again, example.com/members, and you click the logout link and you probably see one on the sidebar on the top, you might not see an easy way to get back in. That is very easily fixed. Log back in by going to example.com/members/wp-admin.

Go to appearance widgets. You will see an area where you can drag what is called WishList Member widgets, from the middle of your screen to the sidebar. Widget is just a fancy term for a block on your sidebar of your site, when you drag this over where you will be able to see that when you view the site again, it displays a logout link. When someone logs out, then there is easy form to fill out to get right back in.

Let us think about what you have added so far to your membership site. You have set it up, added content, protected it, given people the ability to log out and log back in. But now you want to give people the ability to join.

First off, you can add account manually. You can log in to the dashboard, go to WishList members, add new member, and type in anything you want for someone's login name, password, and email address, and create as many of those accounts manually as you want. This means if you want to add access for other business partners or clients, you can, but it is more exciting for us to be able to actually take payments.

I told you that there were tons of choices for even the easiest way to get started is to use a service called PayPal. The reason is because it is very widely used and it is very fast and easy to get started. Just get a business account at paypal.com. Once that it is up and running, go to WishList Member and go to the integration tab, and they will walk you through a step by step process to getting a payment button created.

Once again, there are a few steps but it is only awkward the first time you do it. We will have you set a couple of options in your PayPal account. Then, you will create a button by going to merchant tools, buy now button, and PayPal will have fill in certain things like the name of your product, the price you are going to charge and the WishList will have you copy and paste one or two special codes, so that when someone clicks on the button and buys from you, they get sent to your membership area to create their very own account that they will be able to use login again and again.

If they ever refund, which means they take their money back, or they cancel which means they stopped paying monthly payments, either way, their access is shut off. So there are a few steps involved, but basically you get a PayPal account, go to WishList member integration and follow their instructions. Once the button is created, you then go to grab what is called a button code and back in the frontend of your site, you pasted in as they called action button in the sales letter page.

You have your membership site at /members. You set up your button the exact way that you want it and then you copy the button code from PayPal over to this frontend sales letter which is just at example.com. You paste this in the called action area and now what you have the very simple sales letter, a webpage at example.com, where someone can see headlines with bullet points and reasons to join your site. At the bottom, the logical step for them to take is to click on that, go to PayPal to check out, to pay you money and then they are sent to your members' area.

In PaperTemplate was even an option to add a small tiny link to log in to the membership site if they would ever lost their way. You have your membership site, you have your payment button, and you paste that payment button on your frontend sales letter. That way, if someone wants to buy access to your site, it does not matter if it is $10, $100, or $1,000 a month, they see the reasons to join.

They click the PayPal button. They check out on PayPal and they end up inside your membership site to create their account. In the future, you think you are crazy if you want to create additional levels for your membership site. I told you already that you have this full level.

But in the future, if you ever want to sell additional products within the site, just go to the levels tab of WishList member. Create a new level called whatever the name of this new product is. In our membershipcube site, we do sell access to the entire site. We also sell just one plugin called WP Drip, and that is on a level called WP Drip that has access only to one post in the site.

We sell access to a plugin called WP import plugin, the level is called WP import and only has access to one post in the site. Creating new levels are easy. Just go to levels, admin level and type it in, and then you go to the content tab, choose that new level you have created and check the boxes next to each post to give that level access to those additional posts.

In the spirit of keeping things simple, I would not get too crazy with this membership level until you had paying members on your full level but this is always an offer for you, and it gets a lot of fun when you link to the ability to upgrade.

For example, let us say you had the front page of your site at example.com. Then, you wanted to sell, in our case a plugin called WP import. I could just go to the frontend WordPress site at the root, go to pages, add new, print a new page called /wpimport, and using PaperTemplate, make a whole separate sales letter write that in there just for WP import.

I could create a level in the /members WordPress site. To get people access just to this WP import level, create a host and give that level access, then go to the integration tab and create a payment button, let us say for $7 that integrates just with the WP import level. So, when someone clicks that button, checks it out and pays $7, they are not buying access to the whole site. They are only buying access to that WP import level.

I could place the copy and paste PayPal button code on the WP import sales letter and also adding whatever headlines, bullet points, and sentences I want. If someone goes and finds example.com/wpimport. They go and they buy it and register for an account in example.com/members but they are only on the WP import level. I could then give them the option to upgrade.

I could then link in that members' area directly to a button or link them back to the front page of example.com and give them the ability to read more about it and click the button and buy access to the full level. There are a lot of possibilities here.

If you ever create an updated version 2.0 of your course, you just create it on a new level and give people the ability to buy access to it leaving the original content alone. This makes managing everything light years easier than the old way because you could potentially host hundreds or thousands of products inside the same site. You can give your users an upgrade path and even have a bird's eye view of who is a member of which levels and what needs focusing on in your business.

For now, your number one priority is to get those four modules of content created and post it inside of your members' area. Once that is done, you can get an email autoresponder account by going to aweber.com, create a list, publish a web form that you can get a copy over in the WishList member integration autoresponder tab that when someone joins your membership site, they are then added to an email list and you can contact them as a buyer repeatedly if they need to log in or buy something new from you.

There are possibilities in the future for drip content, but I want you to be careful about this. Be careful about teasing your members too much, and for lying on the monthly drip in order to make money. A drip is nice but as far as I am concerned, the only reason to hold off on some of your content is to avoid overwhelming.

I know, _____ who have the mindset of, "Well, I will just take this 100-page book, cut it up into slices of 10 pages each and give them one chunk per day or one chunk per week." The problem with that is that people think they are buying a 100-page report, they join and they see that they only get 10 pages, and after way wish to get the next small chunk. People are going to be the most excited when they first joined your site, so giving them at the very least some kind of a starter kit and separate the idea between training and reference.

I have a copywriting course, for example, called Speed Copy, which is located inside of WishList member site. If someone wants to know how to write sales letters or persuade people with video webinars, they could join this course and it gives them a step by step process in four modules. But it also maintains things like my split test results, my suite file. Copy critiques have other people's sales letters and these were all things that are not the core components of the course.

They are very valuable. They are very nice to have, but they are on their own separate pages and are not part of the course. I want you to think about that, you have people join your course for the core for the starter kit. If you want to drip out content, you drip out the nice to haves, not the must haves.

The reason why many people have drip content is to reduce refunds. Think about this, if you sold a course with a 30-day refund period which is common with PayPal or a 60-day refund period, which common with a service called Clickbank, it is a good idea to give them one or two or three or more extra things over the course of next few weeks as long as you do not get too carried away.

Think about that, if someone joined your course and immediately had some buyers or more for whatever reason, they might stick around to get access to a bonus in a week, another bonus, another bonus, more things to help them along and guarantee they get results. Having a drip content is good to provide an extra experience, produce refunds but you want to drip out the library components, the add-ons, the goodies and not the core essential elements people need to get that quick result.

I know we touched on a lot of technical terms, details and tools,but I want you to use Namecheap for your domain name, HostGator for your webhosting, WordPress and PaperTemplate at the root of your site for the sales letter. WordPress and WishList member in the members' folder of your site for the member's area, and then get an email autoresponder account using Aweber.com to then integrate your autoresponder with your membership site and PayPal to accept digital online payments for someone to buy access to your site.

We can get to the fanciness like drip and dashboard pages and interaction later but the most important thing right now is to get passed that initial 10%. Get the tip of the iceberg created. Get the site setup in online, so that you can then begin promoting this.

Section 4: Niche & Content

I've had enough. I've had enough of people padding or bloating or loading up their sites, especially membership sites with way too much stuff. Everyone stresses out about content creation and they want to create so much that they've lost sight of what people actually want.

Think back to those first few books or the first few membership sites that you ever joined. If you saw a membership site that was all about how to double the distance that you can shoot the golf ball in a month versus a site with 1,000 different golf tips, you'd probably think that those 1,000 golf tips weren't very good or very focused or weren't really in a clean plan of action. I keep telling you that those people, who are about to buy from you, especially buy into your membership site are frustrated. They're at the end of the rope and they've tried all the other alternatives before you. Most of the other alternatives are either out of date, too complicated or just didn't work.

What's my point? Well, I want you to focus less on adding in and piling in a bunch of stuff and turn your attention instead to getting your content created as fast as possible. Create it as something that would've helped you starting out or would've helped you 1 or 2 years ago and is based in reality. You use one of your own case studies. For example, if you're teaching golf, you show yourself or explain the different techniques that you personally use on the golf game. If you're teaching a course on guitar, actually have a guitar there and record even some audio clips or some pictures or some drawings that actually show you playing the guitar.

Just that alone will differentiate you, in comparison to people who compile articles or research Wikipedia or other videos to try to put together a crappy membership site or a crappy product. I want you to keep a few things in mind. First of all, what's the hook of your membership site? What's your slight, and I did say slight, unique span on solving this common problem of making money from the stock market, playing guitar, improving your golf game and so on? The next thing, if you had to create a 21 to 30 day boot camp, what modules would be in it? What would be the end game result of someone completing that boot camp and what would the weekly milestones of the 4 modules be along the way? The next thing is to record very simple, very easy video.

I come across so many people who stress about the quality of their videos and they think that they need to shoot a live action, green screen, multiple camera, professionally shot clip. Some of these people end up spending 6 months just to record a 1 or 2 hour video. I'm here to tell you that, if I had to choose between a video that was shot in poor lighting but had good quality compared to a video that looked beautiful and was shot with excellent lighting and production but had bad content, of course I'd choose the one with good content and bad lighting.

In this day and age, there's no excuse. You can use a tool called Camtasia to record your screen. It comes with a 30 day trial. You can record live action video, if that's what you want, using an iPhone or an iPod Touch which will run you about $200. Guess what, if you can find some kind of device like that at BestBuy or CostCo store, you can buy it, use it and if you still don't like it or you still can afford it or you still haven't made your money back at the end of that month, you can always return it, right?

What I want to put in your head is for you to create 60-90 minute video modules, and only create 4 of them. If you're stared for content, if you're still new, then even 30-60 minutes are worth but we don't want to go for 2 hours or longer. We also don't want to record simple 5-10 minute videos because it's harder to pack in the real good stuff. That's more appropriate for things like free articles and free blog posts to tease people with content in your membership site. You want to record in video, whether we're talking about screen capture video on your computer screen or live action video using your iPhone.

I'm also not talking just about you sitting in front of the camera and talking, rambling about things. I want you to actually show things. If you're making a real estate course, then recording your computer screen would be fantastic because you could say… "Let's say I have X number of dollars in cash and here are the steps I would do to get a loan online… Here are the steps I would take to narrow down the neighborhood… Here are the steps I would take to, once I have a neighborhood, decide on which foreclosed house I'm going to buy, and then I would look at these factors"

You know what you could actually do? Actually go out and flip a house. You don't necessarily have to go out and film every single step. You don't have to film yourself going out to the house but you could say "I'm about to go out and do this and I'm looking for these 10 criteria" then pause the video or stop the video, go out and do it and then come back and hit the record button again and just go through that list and report on what happened. While everyone else is teaching tips or adding a new thing, you can actually switch between your own personal case study of you apply the system and the rules of the system itself. The system is going to be things like, if you can utilize a certain software or have a step-by-step checklist or just a proven way and proven templates on how to, for example list a house on a real estate market and just give people a very easy, repeatable formula, a process that they can repeat so that they can duplicate your results.

If I have to hear one more time that people buy because they want to consume more and more content. No, they buy from you and they buy the most exciting things because they want to get some results. If you show the way that you got those results and you show yourself doing the results and add in things like accountability and help them along to get the same results, then that is going to be a membership site unlike any other. It's actually you sharing more than just simple information.

Let's step back for a second and talk about the hook of your membership site because any idiot could make a membership site about how to learn Spanish but if you had a way to teach someone Spanish in a couple of weeks. If someone is about to go on a trip and they forgot to study or if they are about to move to a new city or they want to learn Spanish to become more hirable, whatever the reason is, you need to know it and you need to know how everyone else is teaching it. I told you in the past to go to sites like Amazon.com and go to Click Bank. What's really going to help is, for me at least, is to go to Amazon.com especially, look up the books you want and look through the table of contents.

I don't recommend at all that you buy any of these books and read through them and take notes because you know what will happen? Weeks will go by and you still won't have that membership sites. The chances are the topic that you're looking to make your membership site is something where you're already somewhat familiar. If you brought up, for example, 5 books on Amazon about real estate, about flipping a house specifically and you opened up the table of contents and just flipped through, you'd probably notice several similarities and several things that you see in common between these books.

Just so that you have some kind of a finger or the pulse of your market place, look at 5 or 10 of these books and come up with a list of about 10 total topics that they all seem to have in common, that people want, that are actually somewhat exciting. Then what you do is, out of these 10, cross out all but 7 and reorder and rearrange them so that they go in a logical step-by-step format. When someone, even if they're brand new to flipping real estate, by the time they're done, they now know not anything and everything there is to know about flipping real estate but those exact things that they know to do with themselves and follow your exact system.

What's also cool about rearranging this and figuring a few things out is that you'll stumble upon the alternatives and the market trend and the things people have tried in the past, like renting out home or doing some kind of lending or reverse mortgage. You can start thinking of ways to discount or even discredit these other possible ways of making money with real estate. In that way, when someone comes across this sales letter you create with your headline and 10 bullet points, 10 good reasons to buy it from you, you'll almost make fun of or explain away the other possible avenue that person would take so the only thing left to do is go ahead and buy from you.

As you're rearranging, you're figuring out these or so parts of your course, you'll start to think about terms or your own unique spin on things that make it just a little bit different than everyone else. This is called a hook. This is where, you're not just teaching real estate, you're not just teaching how to flip a home, you're helping people who tried in the past to make money with real estate and maybe they've lucked out or they lost money but now, after all this long journey they finally found you and now you're going to show them the simple way, the proven way, the way that's easy and fun and fast and works over and over again.

You have these 10 things, narrowed down to 7 and rearranged. What I want you to do now is combine any of these 7 together so that you have a total of 4 modules. What's really important, and a lot of times when we're planning things and trying to decide on things to remove choice and to put ourselves in a box, in a way. By that, I mean it's easy to say "You should make content. You should just generate…" If you want to make an hours' worth or 5 hours' worth but if I specially tell you that you need to have just 4 modules, no more than 4, no less than 4, that reduces your choices in a good way and now, you're one step closer to completion and you just need to figure out which parts go into which boxes. Whatever niche you're in, whether it's playing piano, playing guitar, stock trading…

In fact, let me just brainstorm a membership site that I may create as someone who teaches how to create websites right now. When I go and look around on places like Click Bank or places like Amazon, I'll see lots of discussion for example about WordPress, WordPress blogs… That's a big one. Things like domain name and website setup is also another big one. Deciding on a niche, building a list, list building, it might be… Traffic and affiliates could be another thing. Let me just list the 10 things that I found just now searching around.

1. WordPress blog, 2. Domain name and website setup, 3. Niche, 4. List building, 5. Traffic and affiliates, 6. Brand, 7. Sales letter and graphics, 8. Backend and upsells, 9. Joined ventures, 10. Services and payment processors. This is just from looking on Clink Bank, looking on sales letters, looking on Amazon table of contents and adding in what I know and I think could be somewhat interesting. That way we have our bases covered, but if we just started with these 10 topics and we create it 10 videos or 10 modules, it would be a long, drawn out, boring course that, let's be honest, we might not even finish because now we have to drudge 10 different things.

Let me first narrow down the 10 to the top 7. We're going to find the 3 weakest in this list and either cross them out or work them into another existing item here. I'm looking through, I see things like niche, I see things like a brand and I think we can combine them. We could talk about your niche and also the branding you're going to use. We need to narrow down one more. I'm looking at domain name and website setup, service and payment processors. We can combine those all into one area, so domain name, website setup, services, payments, processors. We're down to 8. We just need to either cross out one final one or combine them. What I'm seeing is list building and traffic and affiliates, we can combine those.

Now, we have 7 very compact modules. 1. WordPress blog, 2. Domain name, website setup, services and payment processors 3. Niche and brands, 4. List building, traffic and affiliates, 5. Sales letter and graphics, 6. Backend and upsells, 7. Joined ventures. By the way, think back to the forums, the message boards you visited in your niche. If you're still stuck, I would also scroll through the different Google groups or Facebook groups or message boards in your subject. Just searching Google "Real estate space forum, Chess space forum" Don't go through and read the individual messages but scroll through the list of topics, the titles, just to see the recurring nagging issues, the desperate problems that people are actually having.

We reduced 10 items to 7 and now it's time to rearrange them, which I've just done into 1. Niche and brands, 2. Domain name, website setup, services and payment processors, 3. WordPress blog, 4. Sales letter and graphics, 5. List building, traffic and affiliates, 6. Backend and upsells, 7. Joined ventures. If you know anything about internet marketing, you might think it's kind of weird that I talk about traffic in the middle of the membership site and then we get back into fixing up a site and then we finish with joined ventures.

This is the power of actually thinking through the order and the way you rearrange things because you can have a lot of fun with getting people starting quickly, then switching gears, building up this other piece, then switching gears back. That way you're not spending half the time on traffic and half the time on the product. You're moving around in different places and getting people results all along the way.

That's huge. Where you want to have in the back of your minds, what results and what tangibles will someone have as they're going through this course? Will they have this WordPress blog installed by the first night they get this? Will they have 3 blog posts up and running by Module 2 or when they're about a week in? Will they have 10 comments and 20 e-mails opt-ins by the 3rd module and so on.

What we're going to do now is we look at our 7 bullet points or 7 topics but we only want to create 4 modules. We're going to split these up, keeping in mind that these don't split up evenly and that's perfectly okay. You're going to have some modules where you have lots of little topics and other modules where only 1 or 2 topics will fill in the whole, entire thing. We're going to take these 7 topics and push them together into 4 modules.

Looking at this, I think the first module should contain niche and brand, domain name, website setup, payment processors and WordPress blog. That first module is just the setup and once they're done with that first module, once they order our course tonight, they'll not only have their website completely online but they'll also have a simple WordPress site set up, which is where most courses take a month or 2 to get to.

Then for module 2, obviously we're going to start of sales letter and graphics. I think that it would make sense for our module to just have that topic. Sales letter, graphics, copywriting, what to say, what to tweak, how to get it all integrated, that'll work for me. Then for the 3rd module... I think we could have the 3rd module be just list building and traffic, and then the final module will be, I guess we can call them enhancements, improvements, next steps but the final module will contain the backend and the upsells.

Going back and looking at this, you have Module 1: Setup, which tackles the niche and brands, domain names, website, services and payment processors and the WordPress blog. We would talk about this for 60 or 90 minutes. Once they have completed watching that video, then we might have an assignment at the end, which is to set up your WordPress blog. Then for copywriting, we explain sales letter and graphics and what to say and how to make it look so the assignment at the end of that one would be to set up your sales letter. For traffic, list building, affiliates, getting free traffic, paid traffic, SEO pay per click... The assignment there would be maybe to have an opt-in page and some ads. Then, finally enhancements where we add upsells, joined ventures. The assignment there might be just to contact 5 people.

This is, in a lot of ways the exact opposite of how most product creators and membership site creators plan out their content. Instead, most people plan out... "Here's what's coming out Wednesday, Tuesday, Thursday, Friday" and they pile on and pile on, not keeping in mind what people actually want. They're paying you whatever price you charge because what they're paying is less than the value they think they'll get back. If all they're giving them is some ideas and thoughts and tips and things to watch and homework assignments, they're just paying you to get distracted. I'd rather people to pay me to get a result. Sometimes, that's money, if we're talking about stock trading, real estate, internet marketing but it also just might be health or it might be that hobby like guitar or a piano.

I hope that the gears are turning in your head about what will be in the sales letter at some point because now the sales letter almost writes itself because all we basically have to say is, if you want to have a WordPress blog, a sales letter that takes payments, an opt-in page that gets traffic and people aproning you day in and day out, then join this course and I'll show you... I'll not just tell you the exact system to do but I'll show you as I do it and I'll make sure that you do it in addition.

We've planned out this course. The next step is to record it. For this, I definitely recommend that you block out time to do it. Ideally, record these videos, this content on a day where you have nothing else to do in your internet business, where you sit down at a computer, you record the stuff and it's done. If you're really advanced, you could present these live webinars. We showed you how to do that inside of our Membership Cube course but if you're still brand new and starting out, then it's still just perfectly okay to record these videos using Camtasia recorder and then post the videos when you're done.

You want to plan for a 60 to 90 minute presentation. What I like to do is, I like to plan for 60 and then if I tend to go a little overtime, it ends up being 90 minutes. For as the structure of your training itself, for each individual module, I have basically 2 things to throw at you, 2 filters to pass this throw. The first is that it'll make a lot of sense if you, first of all, explain what you're about to do in your video.

I like to just start off with a usual PowerPoint presentation, add some bullet points with the steps they are going to do today, then do the steps and then show that exact, same PowerPoint at the end with the steps that we just took. Explain what you're going to do, do it and then we're going to explain what you just did.

What we have so far is, for example, for the Module 1, for the setup module, I explained the things we're going to talk about like a niche, brand, domain name, WordPress blog so that they get the big picture. Then, we'd actually do it. Then, we explain what they just did and then give them an assignment so that they can do it as well. That's the first filter I want you to look at this.

The second one is a system called WWHW which is why, what, how to, what if. This is basically the way that everyone things and the way that it makes sense and that things will go in a logical, start to finish, step-by-step fashion without getting scouter brain. We start off for the first 5 or 10 minutes explaining the big picture, the really big picture, like why is this important and then the "what" is we're about to do, then the "how to" is, we go through each step and do it and then the "what if" is well now, here's what we just did and what if you did it, here's your assignment.

The "how to" component of this is going to take up most of your session. We're talking about say 40-45 minutes. The "what if" shouldn't take too long, just about 5-10 minutes at the end. The "why" part should just be about 10 minutes and the "what" should be 10-20 minutes. If you were stuck or stressing out a few minutes ago, about how the heck am I going to create a 1 hour video, now that we've broken it down, it's going to be hard to keep your video under an hour, just by explaining the significance of this, why this is so important, what we're about to do, then we do it, making sure that very carefully, very collusive so that everybody understands and then "what if" with the assignment so they can do it as well. Why, what, how to, what if. Why this is important, what are we going to do, how to do it and now what if you do it, the assignment at the end.

The assignment at the end, I like to call them challenges but basically, I list out 4 questions that people have to answer. If you want to be advanced, you can get people the ability to leave a comment and answer those 4 questions but you don't have to but just list 4 things and, by them answering these 4 questions it'll be very clear what needs to happen next. What we'll do is we'll ask 4 questions directly relating to this assignment.

The first question will be some kind of name based thing. This might be, if I'm teaching someone how to record and post a 10 minute video online, it would be "What's the name of your video?" If I'm teaching someone how to create a website, the question is "What's the name of your website?" If this is a real estate course, the name might be "What city are you going to look for a house?" or "What street or a neighborhood will you look for a house?" You want to have a name type of thing.

The next question is going to be some kind of detail. In the video marketing course a detail question might be "How many minutes long will your video be?" Detail question for real estate would be "What price range of a home are you going to buy and flip?" For guitar, it might be "Are you going to buy an acoustic or an electric guitar?" For golf, it might be "What brand of golf clubs...?" The first question is the name question, the second one is a detail question.

The third one is a proof question. This will be a question relating to how are you going to prove to me that this is done. If we're talking about a video, a question might be "What URL will your video be online?" or if it's a website, "What's the URL of the website?" Even in something like a guitar playing or real estate, this proof question would be "Where can I go to see that you've done this?" Maybe, even if I say, "If I search on whatever website that lists homes for sale and I search for this street, is that where I'd find your home listed for sale?" or it might be "What's the link to your

Facebook page, to your Facebook Timeline where you will post the receipt showing that you've bought such and such guitar?"

Then, the fourth question is a deadline, where you just ask "What time and date will this be done?" I highly recommend that you limit people to completing this challenge, this assignment within 7 days of hearing about this. Here's the cool part, it's that right now you're not asking them to go out and do it, you're asking them to commit to you, you're asking them to answer 4 simple questions that'll only take them 2 or 3 minutes to answer.

Like I said, you can just pose the questions to them and they can answer them on their own time or if you happen to have a good number of members in your membership site, you can have them post it as a comment underneath the post where you put the video. We'll get to that in a second.

They're not actually doing it, they're just committing to, which has a nice effect because, first of all, it adds an element of social proof. Even if only 5 or 10 have posted their challenge, that's huge. For someone who joins the site, they'll say "Wow, people are actually using this membership site." The next thing it does, it almost adds some kind of a competition or an accountability because now, if everyone else is completing this and I'm not, I'm left out and also a tiny bit of commitment and consistency because now, I've agreed to do this so I have to follow through.

So, 10 commonalities, narrowed down to 7, rearranged, split up into 4 modules and put each module in a form of "why, what, how to, what if" with the "how to" being the core of it, how to do it and the "what if" being 4 part question, 4 separate questions, a name question, detail question, proof question and a deadline question.

That all sounds well and good but how the heck do you record the video. As I said, Camtasia and/or you iPhone. If you're not that technically skilled, you're still in luck because using this tool called Camtasia Recorder, you can record your entire screen so whatever appears on your screen is what comes out on the finished video. Who cares if someone sees your system clock in the bottom, who cares if people see different icons, just record what needs to be shown and don't worry about the production value. The same is true with an iPhone.

For example, let's say that you're teaching someone how to go to your local Wal-Mart or your local garage sale or a local good will store with a special iPhone app and scan that app and get it listed on Amazon.com for a huge markup. Well, you could just bring in your iPhone, I guess for this you need 2 iPhones, one to record and one to scan but just record yourself going in and doing it. If you were teaching someone how to create an app on the iPhone and or the Android, all you'd have to do is have a logical step-by-step sequence and record your screen, explaining the system and then go through the system yourself for that step, that milestone of you creating your very own iPhone app.

The first part is just recording it. Camtasia Recorder for your screen or an iPhone for a live action video. Camtasia has a 1-click option to upload to YouTube. You might've heard of this, this is the largest video site on the Internet and iPhones also have the same 1-click functionality. I know what you're thinking "But I'm making a site where I'm charging money. I don't want this to be publically available." Well, that's okay because once the site is uploaded, it might take a while, depending on how long the video is… Once it's uploaded, you can edit the video in YouTube and change it from a public listed video to an Unlisted video.

Here's the thing. On YouTube, you can have a site that's public where anyone and everyone can see it or a video that's private where only you can see and then somewhere in between is what's called Unlisted, which means that if someone happens to have the link to the video, it will play for them but it won't be easy for them to find it. If you're technophobic then all you have to do is somehow get that video up on YouTube.

Screen capture or live action, get it on YouTube, change it to Unlisted and then there's a share link for that video. With WordPress, all you have to do is just go to Post, Add New, add the title of the post and then past in the YouTube share link and it will place the video right there in your members area.

You can always make things better later. Later on in the future, if you want to use our video player plugin or some other video service, you can but for now, let's keep it simple and let's get your site online as fast as possible and get all of your content finished. While everyone else is painstakingly editing and scripting out what to say and adding in tips, instead, you're solving problems, you're providing a formula, a system to get someone from point A to point B to point C to point D, where D is that they've now gone through this 20 or 30 day boot camp and now they've discovered how to flip a house, play a guitar, trade in the stock market, install a website, you name it.

Content creation doesn't have to be hard, doesn't have to be a lot of work. You know what? In my experience, the times I've spent a month planning something out, as opposed to a day or an hour it hasn't come out any better. The times where it was taking me a month to record a video that could've taken me a day, it didn't come out any better. Give that some mind. It's that it doesn't have to be perfect, it never will be perfect and it's going to make the most sense to you if you create this while you're actually doing it, while you're excited and you do it in a short timeframe. That way, you're completely focused and you know exactly what you're doing.

Section 5: Niche & Content

Avoid putting the cart before the horse. Here's what I mean. I see quite a few marketers and business owners who want to have the latest, greatest, and the best of everything. They don't want to so-called "waste time" setting up a simple, single-payment, four-module site. They want to skip ahead and make the $20-a-month site and get the entire world involved. They want to wait launching their site and wait putting it out into the world because they want to get everything just right and all the pixels and line perfectly lined. They want to add the upsells and the downsells, the forums that are built-in, the social sharing, and all this monthly content with no idea if people will actually respond to it.

Here's a newsflash most people want. Whatever your crazy idea is, I would appreciate if you put that on hold until the base is built. People will pay you money in exchange for having a problem solved usually in a form of a four-module course. What's great about all this is that if you have a service to provide, for example, if you are a copywriter, then great. You can have a payment button built inside of your membership site where somebody can hire you now that they know that you know what you're talking about.

I know quite a few people who start off with this base membership site. When they want to provide services like setting-up WordPress installations or customizing scripts, they use the skills they developed in creating that four-module course to provide one-time Done-for-You services or even coaching where they record whatever activity they perform. Even if they're posting it on YouTube as an unlisted video or posting on Vimeo PRO or sell closing it themselves, they place that video online, adding

WordPress post to display the video inside the site, and set that membership level to only be available to one single person.

Think about this. My name is Robert Plank. Let's say that someone named Lance Tamashiro bought a one hour copywriting critique from me. A program where for $5000, I will bring up their webpage in my web browser on my computer screen and record for exactly 60 minutes exactly the things I would change on that sales letter to make it convert higher and be more profitable.

The great thing about providing coaching or Done-for-You services in this way is that you're not on anyone's clock. You aren't paid by the hour. You can do this whenever you have an hour or so free. I can open up this webpage in a web browser, record my computer screen using Camtasia recorder, post it on YouTube, create a new post and call it "Lance Tamashiro Consulting Session," create a new membership level called "Lance Tamashiro" and add this post as the only post available for the Lance Tamashiro level. Then I create a new user in this site and his name is Lance Tamashiro. I add in a randomly made-up password, I enter in his email address - that way he will get that login information - and I add this Lance Tamashiro user to a level called "Lance Tamashiro."

I can basically do this for hundreds, if not thousands of clients. Whether they're one-time or recurring coaching clients, whether I'm recording Done-for-You services or meeting with them, I can even give them a recording of the meeting that we had.

You can always add on to this base you built in your membership site. I want you to avoid putting the cart before the horse because it's all about baby steps and stair-stepping you to that first sale, the next sale, and the next level of income that you want.

We're going to talk today about five simple tools that you'll be able to use and plug into your membership site to make it different. That's what you're after, isn't it? You're fighting the anxiety and the nervousness that comes with putting your product out there. A lot of people default on waiting and procrastinating because they feel like this makes them feel better because they're making everything just right. Nothing will ever be "just right" so instead, let's focus on whatever milestones you want to have, whether that's number of members in the site or your level of income.

The tools we're going to talk about today are Video Player, WP Notepad, WP Kunaki, WP-Stats Pro, and WP Drip. Video Player like it sounds like is a player for videos. Whether these are live action or screen capture video, it doesn't matter. WP Notepad is the simple way for your users to take notes and check off items in a checklist. There's a really neat twist on this which you'll see in a little while. WP Kunaki allows you to gather physical mailing addresses.

For some reason, a lot of marketers think that they can have a crappy site. But with one gimmick, everyone will love it. For example, a site with a bunch of crappy tips in it, but because of price is so low, who wouldn't want it? Or some thrown together videos, but because I'm mailing out these videos in a book or in a DVD disc, no one will ever cancel, and that's simply not the case. So if you think that having a physical book or a DVD is going to save you, it's not.

The thing most people don't tell you about having a $20 per month magazine or a $10 per month "DVD of the month" club is that this is expensive. More often than not, you would want to download and display and have these items available digitally instead of physically because anyone can view tons and tons of videos without having to fumble around with discs. They don't have to wait to receive these items in the mail, and it costs you a heck of a lot less because you're basically paying fractions of the penny in bandwidth cost anytime someone wants to watch one of your videos.

But getting a physical address is great if you want to send out a bonus like a one-time DVD set or a book or even a simple thank you card. There are lots of ways to do that, but the WP Kunaki plugin will collect the physical mailing addresses of all your members. WP-Stats Pro allows you to spy on your members and see who is accessing what content. WP Drip allows you to drip out some content overtime whether that's monthly, daily, weekly or anywhere in between - and it's all very simple.

Let's back up for a second. Video Player plugin. I told you before that the easiest and simplest way for you to get content inside the membership area, especially if you're technically challenged, is to upload it to YouTube, right within Camtasia recorder. Heck, if you're not recording your screen, that's still okay because if you're recording using a device like an iPhone or an Android, they have the capability to directly upload to YouTube using their interface.

Once the video is on YouTube, you can quickly edit it by changing the access settings from public to unlisted. Now the video is not publicly available on the Internet, you can grab the share code and place it in your member's area. That will do the job for you for now. If you get to the point where YouTube just isn't cutting it, you can get our Video Player plugin by going to MembershipCube.com.

Here's what the Video Player plugin does. You can either upload your videos in your WordPress site directly in the plugin or if you have a lot, you can transfer them using a thing called FTP or your control panel's File Manager. Whatever way you use to get those videos on your web server, you can click a button, browse for the video and it will display it right there in the video post. None of this crazy messing with permissions or using this thing called Amazon S3. It simply has a link, someone clicks on it, and your video appears right in front of them - very simple.

The only tricky part is that when you are posting the videos yourself, you have to be careful about the size and the quality of the video. Because you can easily have a high quality video, but the problem with a high quality video is that the size of the video will be huge. If you're uploading a 10-minute video, that's 3 gigabytes in size. I'm sorry, that video will look great but it will take hours for people to download and view and it will eat up your bandwidth cost. But if you make a really small-sized video, it won't look very good.

The good news is that the reason I recommend using Camtasia recorder for processing your videos is because it has a web-based setting. If you're at all technically detailed, I prefer to process Camtasia videos that are 1024 pixels wide and 600 pixels high. Camtasia has a quality setting. I set that at about 50%. That it's a pretty decent size video if you're looking to create a video that's between 1 and 2 megabytes per minute in size. That means we have a 10-minute video. If it's a screen capture video, it should be about 10-20 megabytes in size. This ensures that it's a good enough quality but small enough size and we'll be able to view that instantly.

Also make sure you produce the video in what's called an MP4 format. Camtasia lets you produce videos in all kinds of formats. It sounds like a good idea but it's really confusing. You don't want to create a Flash video or a QuickTime video or an iPhone video. You want to create an MP4 video. The good news for this is that with MP4 videos you'll get the best quality with the smallest file size and it will even play on mobile devices if that's something you care about.

The Video Player plugin is available from MembershipCube.com. I prefer to use Camtasia. Even if I'm recording a live action video, I still will drag that MP4 file into Camtasia. That way I can perform edits and cut out the beginning and end, add music if I want, and add text. Even if it's a live action video or a screen capture video where I've recorded my screen, Camtasia makes a great video editor. You can save it out to an MP4 file that's small enough to be displayed on the web.

That's as simple as it needs to be. It's as complicated as it needs to be, too. When we create training courses, and we have a four-module area, we'll create four posts and each post will contain a video. Underneath the video, we might list a challenge and we give people the ability to leave a comment under that module, but that's all the complexity that they need. In the future, what we sometimes will use is the Vice Versa plugin to convert these posts into pages.

There's a plugin called TablePress to draw out a nice looking table and allow people to click on the things they want and it will go to that page or even view the video right there on the page if that's what we want. But that might be a little more advanced for you and if that's the case, please join MembershipCube.

We'll show you how to create a dashboard table using Video Player. If you want something simple for now, which I recommend, make four posts in your member's area. Make sure they're protected and the full level has access to those. Place each video on each post and it doesn't need to be any more complicated than that.

With every decision that I make, I ask myself, "Is taking this action going to make me more money or is it going to make me less money?" If the only thing holding me up is the video player I'm going to use to host my videos, then putting it on YouTube will make me more money because it will actually make sales. If the video being hosted on YouTube looks too unprofessional or it's holding me back from making the amount of money I want and moving from YouTube to a self-hosted Video Player plugin will make me more money, then it makes more sense to do that. Or it might make more sense to face up the sales letter or get more traffic.

Anyway, I'm getting ahead of myself. Let's talk about WP Notepad which is another great bang for your buck and an easy way to turn your member's area from a boring download page to an almost interactive membership site.

I'm not sure how familiar you are with WordPress. But by default, every page or post you create in the site will have a comment area and you can always turn this off by editing the post. You have a piece of content, you have a written article or a video inside the member's area, and underneath, there's usually area for someone to add publicly their comments. They can go and ask a question relating to your training or show what result they have or have their challenges. By the way, inspecting your challenges makes for great case studies and testimonials to put back in your sales letter.

But people can leave comments publicly. The thing that WP Notepad does is add a different box above the comments. This is below the content but above the comments. This is a private note-taking area for the member looking at your site. This means that if I have a membership site about golf and Lance Tamashiro joins this site, he will see a private note-taking area and he can write in whatever notes he wants. That means if he's making bullet point notes about what he's watching, or types in the time and minute that he left off like "I watched the video for 5 minutes and 30 seconds," or needs to remember something for later, or even create a to-do list before that video, he can make these notes but no one else can see them.

For example, Jason Parker also joins the site. He won't be able to see Lance's notes but he will be able to create his own notes. By default, WP Notepad places this note-taking box underneath all of your posts but of course you can customize which ones it does and does not show on. But it doesn't stop there because with WP Notepad, you can also create fill-in-the-bank forms.

We have a site called MakeAProduct.com. This is a membership site - a training course that shows people how to outsource a very important task called dictation. They can speak out articles, books, and more. In fact, that's what I'm doing right now. There are different tools that are used in this process - tools for the hiring process, tools for brainstorming the perfect article. What we like to do is have fill-in-the-blank areas where someone can type in things like their niche or type in things like their website, and it will create a template based on that.

Think about how cool this is if you were teaching real estate. You could provide with someone all the necessary forms they needed to do real estate deals, give them the fill-in-the-blank areas for their own names, and they can print them out. If you're giving someone any kind of business in a box, legal forms, recipes, you name it, you can provide this fill-in-the-blank system and that's built into WP Notepad.

Notepad also allows you to place checklists on whatever post that you want. Let's say you had a course on how to put a video online, how to market your business with a video. You could have a checklist, for example, one checkbox could be to plan your video. One checkbox could be to record the video. Another one to upload, another one to market it, and you can place as short or long as a list of checkboxes that you want and people can check off the checkboxes. Once again, they only see their own checkboxes. No one else sees them so they can keep track of their own progress through the course.

Heck, with WP Notepad, you can even place a completed checkbox. If you had four posts in your site, they could watch the first video and check off that they've completed watching that video or performing that task. Then they can come back months later and pick up exactly there they've left off because you gave them the ability to check off the tasks that they were performing.

Here's the very unique twist in WP Notepad. You can spy on your own members. They can't spy on each other but you, as the creator and the administrator of this site, can see a list of all the posts and tasks that were checked off in your site, all the fill-in-the-blank forms that were filled-out, and the notes that people took.

I find this very helpful to see where people get stuck in my training course. Sometimes I need to go and add in a few extra instructions. Or I like to see how far people get in the course because if I see that everyone has checked off module one and module two, but almost no one has done module three, it might mean that I need to change the instructions or even adjust my autoresponder follow-up sequence or send a broadcast email to my members telling them to go to module three and even ask them why they are stuck. Either way, Notepad is a very easy plugin. That's in MembershipCube. You can install on top of your WishList Member site and begin to not just give your members the ability to take notes but give them fill-in-the-blank forms, checklists, and track everyone's progress.

I know this simple but powerful plugin, WP Kunaki. All this plugin does is place a pop-up on the front page of your membership site when people login. Someone might login for the first time in a long time or they might have bought access to your site. We don't want to make people fill out tons of information before they buy. We want them to buy as fast as possible preferably using PayPal or a credit card or whatever merchant account you use.

Once someone has created their account for login and they've logged in, a pop-up will appear where they can confirm their address. It might be filled in or it might not from your payment process, which sometimes passes this information along. But either way, they can correct or fill in their most current address right in front of you.

This pop-up won't appear every single time they click it on your site, but every time they visit that front page or homepage in your membership site, this pop-up will appear. They can choose to ignore it and click away (and they could go away) or they can fill in the details and click to confirm their address. Now that pop-up will not appear ever again because they've confirmed and verified their address.

Here's what happens after they click that button. First of all, you get an email notification as the administrator of the site letting you know that that person has filled in their details such as mailing address, city, state, zip code, or phone number, and so on. You can do whatever you want with this information. Sometimes, depending on the site, I will use service called Kunaki and I will paste their address into the service and send them something like a CD in the mail or a DVD of a quick start video.

This service called Kunaki is not very user-friendly but you can actually upload a set of discs. You can have a 10-disc set, and as soon as you see that order come in, you can order them a 10-disc set that will be sent to them in the mail automatically after the order is placed. I know what you're thinking. "I don't want to have to process every single email that comes in." You can either have a virtual assistant do it and have email posters[?] that forward it into them or you can login to the backend area of WP Kunaki and dump a list of all your members' addresses.

Of course if you have multiple levels, you can narrow that down - only dump people who have confirmed their shipping details or only dump people who registered this week or this month or last month. The point is that this is an address collector so that you can get people to confirm their address. Guess what, once you sent them that DVD, you can check that you have shipped to them and this will even help you keep track of who still needs something in the mail and who doesn't.

I use a service sometimes called Lulu.com to print and mail printed books. You might use CreateSpace for this and you might even use a service called SendOutCards.com which you can join by going to DoubleAgentCards.com. You can customize your very own thank you card and have it sent out. You can send people a letter in the mail. You can send them brownies, teddy bears, all kinds of crazy stuff. But the point is that WP Kunaki collects this person's mailing address and even phone number if you want.

Think about this. Wouldn't it be great or at least somewhat useful to have a list of all your members' phone numbers? If you want to call them up or use a text blast or a voice blast service such as CallLoop.com and tell them, "Thanks for signing up"? Or maybe if people end up refunding or cancelling from your site, you can give them a phone call to see what happened. Even if you're not at the point yet to send phone calls or make phone calls, you can still have these phone numbers on hand in case you need them.

WP Stats Pro - another easy one to get set-up and another one available inside MembershipCube. It tracks your members' activity on your site. It gives you a long list of most recent people who have logged in, clicked around, viewed different webpages, and how long they've remained on different webpages. One thing I've noticed is that quite a few remembers would login at night and leave the web browser open for 8-10 hours, even sometimes days before they actually do anything. Good information to know.

WP Stats Pro will also show you the activity narrowed down the one single user if you want. So if you're curious to see if someone has even logged in or to see the last time someone has logged in and what and what they did, or even if they're passing around their account details. You can see their IP address, so if they logged in from different cities, countries, continents, then you know that they might be passing this around. If they say that they were never able to access the content, you can see that they have. You can see how far they've gone as far as their progress.

Think about this. WP Notepad will allow people to check off the activities they've completed. But not everyone will do that. You can see if someone has viewed different modules but not necessarily checked it off. Or if they keep going back to our module day after day after day, they might be stuck. You can also narrow down the activity based on one single page or post. You can see from module four a list of everyone who has recently been on the page or the post for module four and how long they stayed there. All very useful stuff to fight refunders, to see how popular some of your posts are, to prevent sharing, and get a good gauge on the difficulty of your membership site.

I saved probably the best plugin for last and this is called WP Drip. For some reason, everyone's dream is to setup a membership site where the entire world buys, the whole world pays $10 or $20 a month and they get a piece of content every week or a few times a month.

This all sounds good in theory but if you ask me, that's creating a chore for yourself. That's creating a lot of extra work for what might not have a bunch of members. But if you want to run a site like this that charges month after month after month - I don't know what you're niche is or your offer or you situation, and heck, if you see a lot of competitors doing something similar and charging on the monthly basis - then you can have your own spin on it and you can do a better job of presenting whatever this training course is.

For example, Lance and I have a couple of sites. One is called Webinar Crusher and one is called Double Agent Marketing where people do pay a monthly fee to meet with us once a month on a group call. This is really cool because we have a recurring webinar scheduled in our calendar, a recurring webinar scheduled in our GoToWebinar service, and we have some scheduled posts that give people the registration link to attend that live call that month. Then we can record the call and place it in the member's area. All we have to do is show up one hour per month and answer questions. If we have 10 or 100 or 1000 members, there's no extra work because we're still showing up for that one hour per month. The difference is how much money we make. That's some pretty cool leverage.

That's one kind of a membership site. If you happen to be in some kind of a niche where you give content, give tools, give information month after month after month then WP Drip is for you.

I'll give you an example. When I first met my business partner Lance Tamashiro, he had a resell rights site called TheMRRClub.com. Lance's site was called TheMRRClub.com. People bought this site to receive what are called resell rights, to receive ready-made businesses in boxes where they could get for example a weight loss business. They could get a weight loss e-book with videos, download pages, pre-written emails, pre-written sales letter, and they would be given the rights to resell this, to place this product on their very own web server, web host or website, and then take payments, bring in money, and keep 100% of the profits.

How cool of a deal is that? To be able to pay money and get a product already created. The thing about The MRR Club is that this was I believe a $37-a-month site. When you joined, you'd receive a couple of hundred of these read-made businesses already and they'd be dripped out over time, over a period of several months, and on and on. These products might cost $5, $20, $50, $100 or even hundreds of dollars on their own, but they were available in one unified and central member's area. They can login and see what new stuff there was. It was all categorized in different niches or based on if you received what are called resell rights, master resell rights, or private label rights (which I won't get into). There are different licenses or different things that people were allowed to do with these products. Because of a plugin like WP Drip, Lance was able to drip these items out over time.

Here's what's really cool about drip content. There are two types, first of all. You could first built-in or setup in WordPress what are called scheduled posts. If today was January 1st, you could schedule a post for February 1st with no extra plugins. You go to add a new post and where you can change the settings in your post after adding the title and the content whether that's written materials, files, or videos, you can change the date that the post is published from immediately writing out today, into either a date in the past to make it backdated or into the future. If today was

January 1st, and you were going to make a post with some weight loss for private label rights content, you could change the date to the future to February 1st. On February 1st, at the exact time you specified, that post or page would now suddenly become live to everyone. You can do the same thing on March 1st, April 1st, June 22nd, or November 7th - you get the idea. That's scheduled content.

With drip content, you can setup a sequence and you can say, "When someone first joins my site, they see this one post." In seven days, they can then see this next post, and in 30 days, they can see another post, and on and on. I have some sites, to be honest, that drip out content for years. I have one site called SpeedCopy.com.

With SpeedCopy, I incorporated a lot of the things we've talked about with membership sites. I had a four-module course to get people from point A to point B. I added in my tools like swipe files. I had a reference library like different sites I created. What's really cool is I've recorded my own byproduct. If I was going to create a new sales letter or juice up an existing sales letter that I already had, I'd record it and explain what I was doing as I was doing it which may not be a very great how-to-step-by-step course but great reference content off of the side.

One thing I also did as part of this course was I critiqued different people's sale letters. I gave them access to those privately. But overtime, those critiques became live to everyone else on the site. How cool is that? Someone pays a one-time fee of $500 to get my tools, my training all at once, even some of the reference material, but then new things came out every month or a few times a month for years to come with no further payments. Why I'm going to do this? First of all, to reduce refund, to get people to keep logging in and keep using the site in addition to things like Kunaki, with a physical bonus, in addition to things like Notepad to help them organize and keep track of things, in addition to WP-Stats Pro to spy on members and see what they were doing. This WP Drip plugin allowed me to create a sequence, give them a bunch of content up front and more over time.

What's really cool about this is if you had a single payment site and you decided in the future to change it up to a monthly site where someone pays month after month after month, you're going to do two things. First of all, install WP Drip and rearrange the dates on the posts so that it shows the first piece of content up front. The distance in time that your posts are spaced out means that that's how soon or how slow the content will come out. So if you have one post per week scheduled in your site and it's all live right now, then by installing drip, it will give people the first days with a content and then it will give them day 7, day 14, day 21, and so on, the longer they're on your site.

The only weird part to get your head around is that different members will see different things. One member who just joined today will see different content than the member who has been in for six month because they see more stuff as time goes on. WP Drip even changes the date that appears on your various posts so that it appears fresh and new. So if you have posts on January 1st, February 1st, and March 1st, and someone joins on June 1st, that first post will look as if it was added to the site on June 1st. The next post will appear as if it was added on July 1st and so on.

I said that the first step was to install WP Drip so that your content is dripped out. The second step is to login to PayPal and create a new payment button. Before, I told you to create a "Buy Now" button so that you can take one single payment like $7, $100, or $1,000 and when someone paid, they get access, if they refund, they're kicked out. In PayPal, you can create what's called a "Subscription" button which is a fancy term for saying that you will accept multiple payments over time.

What you can do is create a "Subscription" button in PayPal that is, for example, $100 every 30 days forever. Depending on how you set things up, you can change one other setting in PayPal when you make that button and charge $100 every 30 days for five payments, and then it's completely paid off. Either way, the membership site WishList Member only cares if this member is someone in good standing, which means that if they paid one time and didn't hear anything else from PayPal, then great, they still have access. If they paid and refunded, then their access is cut off. If they paid all five payments and there's no other news to report, great, they still have access. If they made only four out of five payments and then cancelled their subscription, which means they will no longer be billed, then WishList cuts off their access. If they're paying month after month after month after month forever, and after 12 months, they cancel their subscription, WishList gets the notification from PayPal and cuts off their access.

Drip allows you to space out your content and changing the button in PayPal allows you to have recurring content. There are all kinds of extra bells and whistles in Drip that I don't want to get into right now, but you can exclude a level or a category from your drip sequence, which means that you can give a VIP level access to everything up front.

In the past, I've had buttons side by side where for $500 they get access to the entire site, even drip content all at once. Or for five payments of $100, they get their starter kit and things are dripped out overtime. The thing I want you to remember is to be very careful of not dripping enough content on people. You need to give people at least some kind of a starter pack. You can't just take a long one hour video and cut it up into ten equal segments and give people minutes 1 through 6 on day one, minutes 7 through 13 on day two - that doesn't work. What instead would work out is if you gave someone access to a complete step-by-step system on day one and gave them more things overtime - extra tools, extra bonus calls - but give them something complete to buy into right now.

A common trap you need to avoid is to drip out a course that only lasts 30 days. No one appreciates that. To buy into something and they get something on day 1, day 2, day 7, day 10, day 20, day 30 - that doesn't work. What you need to do is give people whatever a month's worth of content is up front. They buy into a complete system, they get all of that up front, and you might drip out a couple of things once a week. But those are extra supplement of materials, if that makes sense.

Use drip as a powerful tool to keep people on your site, prevent them from refunding, but be very careful about going overboard on the drip or hoping that putting the cart before the horse will save you or hoping that polishing that turd will make it a better turd, it won't. But if you start off with a simple base and add these tools on, like a Video Player, WP Notepad, WP Kunaki, WP-Stats Pro, and WP Drip, then I'm very confident that you'll have a site that you'll enjoy creating and maintaining that others will also have a lot of fun using, consuming, and paying for again and again. But start simple and add on to it from there.

About the Author

Robert Plank runs a million dollar business on the Internet creating information products, software tools, and webinar training.

He can show you how to not only save time in your business and everyday life, but do more in less time. Master WordPress. Build your list. Create passive income from information products. Generate residual income using membership sites. Scale and talk to use audiences using webinars. And more!

Robert's Online Presence:

- Blog: www.robertplank.com
- Podcast: www.robertplankshow.com/itunes
- Fan Page: www.robertplankshow.com

Robert Plank's other titles on Amazon.com:

- 100 Time Savers: Start Less, Finish More, and Cut 10 Minutes a Day from Your Schedule to Gain 60 Hours of Free Time Per Year
- Article Crash Course: Get Published, Get Instant Authority and Become an Expert in Any Subject
- Double Agent Marketing: Live the Double Life, Control Your Destiny and Become a Self-Employed Entrepreneur By Starting Your Own Home-Based Internet Information Business
- Four Daily Tasks: Overcome All Internal Roadblocks Using a Few Simple Rules, Solve Any Personal Problems and Keep Moving in a "Forward" Direction in 10 Easy Steps

- Internet Marketing on Crack: Master Your Time Management, Marketing, Sales, Traffic, Products, Customer Relationships & More From Just a Few Simple Breakthroughs
- List, Traffic & Offers: The Internet Marketing Profit Shortcut
- Membership Cube: How to Create a Passive Income in Just a Few Simple Clicks
- Secret Conversations with Internet Millionaires: How to Make Money Online with an Internet Marketing Business
- Sell on Amazon FBA: Easy Steps to Create an Online Passive Income Amazon Business with Retail Arbitrage & Private Label Sourcing
- Setup a Point & Click Website Today: Install WordPress, Create Massive Content, Secure and Backup Your Blog WITHOUT Being a Computer Geek

Robert's courses:

- Membership Cube: setup a recurring membership site
- Income Machine: establish your online system including your blog, traffic, opt-in page, autoresponder sequence and more
- Dropship CEO: sell physical products on Amazon.com
- Make a Product: self-publish a book (physical and digital) on Amazon.com
- Profit Dashboard: earn money from Fiverr
- Podcast Crusher: create your own podcast

Discover more about him at RobertPlank.com/about and contact him at RobertPlank.com/ask if you have a personal question, want to appear on his podcast, want him on your podcast, or if you wish to enquire about availability for speaking engagements.